because
why

because why

POEMS

Sarah Fox

COFFEE HOUSE PRESS

MINNEAPOLIS

2006

Coffee House Press books are available to the trade through our primary distributor, Consortium Book Sales & Distribution, 1045 Westgate Drive, Saint Paul, MN 55114. For personal orders, catalogs, or other information, write to: Coffee House Press, 27 North Fourth Street, Suite 400, Minneapolis, MN 55401.

Coffee House Press is a nonprofit literary publishing house. Support from private foundations, corporate giving programs, government programs, and generous individuals help make the publication of our books possible. We gratefully acknowledge their support in detail in the back of this book.

Good books are brewing at coffeehousepress.org

LIBRARY OF CONGRESS
CATALOGING-IN-PUBLICATION DATA

Fox, Sarah
Because why / Sarah Fox.
p. cm.
Poems.
ISBN-13: 978-1-56689-186-8 (alk. paper)
ISBN-10: 1-56689-186-8 (alk. paper)
I. Title.
PS3606.O9565B43 2006
813'.6—DC22
2005035800

FIRST EDITION | FIRST PRINTING
1 3 5 7 9 8 6 4 2
Printed in the United States

The poem "Myrtle" cites *King's American Dispensatory*, by Harvey Wickes Felter, M.D., and John Url Lloyd, Phr.M., Ph.D. (1898).

Acknowledgments

Thanks to the editors of the following magazines and anthologies in which some of these poems originally appeared: *Bloomsbury Review, Conduit, The Drunken Boat, Elixir, Forklift: Ohio, Fuori:one, Fuori:two, Jacket, jubilat, Knuckle Merchant, Muse Apprentice Guild, Post Road, PuppyFlowers, Shattered Wig, Spinning Jenny, Spout, Swerve,* and *Verse.*

Much appreciation to the following organizations whose generous support enabled me to do this work: the Bush Foundation, the National Endowment for the Arts, the Minnesota State Arts Board, and the Jerome Foundation.

For their various forms of encouragement, faith, and sustenance, I am grateful to my parents, Paul and Susan Fox, and my siblings, Paul, Margaret, Chris, Peter, and Annie; Michaelyn Bachhuber, James Fox, Dina Goodwill, Kimberly Hart, Carolyn Holbrook, Christopher Jones, Terry Kohlmeier, Eric Lorberer, Cris Mattison, Sigrid Nichols, Theo Page, Michela Anita Papadia, Patrick Scully, Tamara Tinkham, Allan Kornblum and everybody at Coffee House Press, and especially my beautiful daughter, Nora Catherine Wynn.

xoxo to Julia, Grace, Milo, Luke, Donovan, Eva, Chloe, Rory, Felix, and Finn.

And abundant gratitude to all of my friends and comrades whose insight is inseparable from the making of this book, in particular: Paula Cisewski, John Colburn, Brian Engel-Fuentes, Melanie Figg, Lisa Fink, Steve Healey, Ted Mathys, Rachel Moritz, Amanda Nadelberg, and Fred Schmalz.

The greatest debt is owed to Chris Fischbach.

Contents

when god decided to invent
everything he took one
breath bigger than a circustent
and everything began

when man determined to destroy
himself he picked the was
of shall and finding only why
smashed it into because

—E.E. Cummings

because John

Guidebook for a Pleasant Stay

Don't speak!

Shade your eyes, Brother.
Face the dawn.

Fuse the bones of the dawn
with the bones of the dove,
feed your emperor.

      Are you experienced.

          Blame it on the dawn.
              The dove of the interior.
         Antidote.   Are you confused.

Go ask Mary Shelley.
Go try to be harmless.

          Sit in the corner through a string of bad years.
            Eating bones at night in the thicket,
            I made an absence.

     Be static, tree.
     Treasure your pharmaceutical acclaim.

Vote today. Vote for me! Vote for elevators. Vote for a whirligig.
   Shave your legs.

Take the high road, the hard road. Take your medicine.
    My hands over the years have been replaced
    by my father's. The crooked index. A scalpel. Their prayer.

Clean your room!
Enjoy your Orlando Disney vacation.
Reading your mind, become downtrodden.
                      If only everything could talk.

Listen to me.

Don't let that punk rake your lawn. Lock the doors.
Damn it!
Do your science. Do the math.
Look at me. Will you just honey look at me once.

Turn that down! Close the window. Cover it up.
That's a dead bird you know. In case you haven't noticed.

Pay attention.

Grab a drink.

Increase your waiting your limits your situational disabilities
    your dosage.
Your shitload your brain waves your airtime.
Eliminate continents of wonder.

                      God save the queenie.
                      Fatten up your pet baby.

Those children, those lovers,
those fucking punks.
Fuck you!

Feel free to wonder around.
You should draw on your yoga.
Sigh from my cigarette.
Love your mother.
Love the Earth and its creatures love love and war and television
and its heroes.
Change your mind.

Buy your baby a mockingbird, five golden rings, a reliable assort-
ment of firearms.

Go tell it on the mountain. Go tell it to the man.
I'm going to tell your father.

It's time to go.
Your heart is ablaze in the soil.
Wait up!

Naturally the word is the beginning
of the end, and in the beginning
was the word's fault.

Come stray in the fog's hypnotic acre,
become the beginning of the ghost
with a word on the tip of his collar.

The last word is always
a fable,

comforting   nowhere.

Find your sister. Wear your seatbelt. Call home Sundays.

Pick up those shoes. Answer the question.
Use complete sentences. Turn off the lights.

Now. Now. Now. Now. Now!

Look it up. Get a fucking life lady.
Don't count on it. Be careful.
Live richly.
Watch your language.

1

Liberation Initiative #27

There was a boy who blew up
trains. You read about him,
he's so notorious and uncaught
with his quarters, his invisible shoelaces.

One day you find yourself
on a train with the boy
who blows up trains.

>"What's that coming out of your eyes?"
>   Hold on a second, I'm trying to finish this story.

You decide to turn him in
when you spy him heading
for the phone booth. In fact
it's a set up you had nothing
to do with—the cops unfold,
the people coo and sigh and cheer.
The boy is shackled. He's in clear view
when you realize, suddenly,
that boy is your lover! You
push through the crowd and reach for him:
"I guess I won't be seeing you for a while."

Later in the lounge car the art historian
does a stand-up shtick in French.
Perhaps you even are in France.
Perhaps now something will really happen.

You remember: *nice belly, nice belly*.
You'll miss him!

You begin describing his escapades
in detail to classrooms across the nation:
complex telephone networks, covert
implants, the unique language understood
only by the culprit and his parrot
that you've managed to decode
for the homeland security specialists.
A thorough deconstruction job by job.

        "Hey, wait a minute."
        I lost my patriot badge in Rome!
        I thought we were safe and still in France!

That's when it all comes rushing back.
"The boy," the story, the train, the match.
The last figment annihilated: no place left to hide.

Fool's House

The longest captivity still carries a familiar tempo.
Sometimes
          you are wrong.

My true love approaches with a grain of sand
he has found for me.
My true love with his open
hand captures all the insects for me.

My margins are leaking again.
My true love follows me around.

When I moved my belongings to this new place
they disguised themselves
as different things entirely.
Thus am I belittled each morning
when I find I've forgotten their names.

Every bird here distrusts me.
It's not so great!
I believe each bird is glass.
This aids me in my feelings.

From morning till night, helicopters
circle our home.
Little field animals and cats
and ants evacuate the yard.
Poor things!

I've forgotten the words to the chant
that worked so well the last time.

I still recognize a sensation occasionally
such as "tumble" or "evaporate" or
"yellow, red," etc.
But I no longer "have an idea."

Habits form that must be quit.
I am now in the middle of my life,
like a bull's-eye.
I learn not to be embarrassed.
Verily I say unto myself, I've turned into
exactly what I've always been.

What do you do with the mad that you have?

> *I'm trying to make a rainbow with a flashlight*
> *and a water sprayer.*
> *I hope it works!*

The solution has something to do with foresight,
which I've gained at the expense of vocabulary.

Here is the calendar. Here is the scrapbook.
Here is the moment. Am I in bed?
My true love sleeps in a ring.
My true love waters the garden.
He is so much more than I seem.

Notice the cloudless sky!
The sky at twilight: each time
a bewilderment.
Exposing the random ethos of our museums.
Did you, like me, always mistake the corsage for our mother?

It is easier to describe things by what they are not.
I am not: sunny, unmistakable, unremarkable, akin.
The day is not: any cloud, birdless, chilly.
And so on,
to meals, pens, trees, what have you.

Someone—*you suspect yourself*—has confiscated
the key. You remember a click,
an engine aroused. You remember once responding
in an interview, "The first thing I remember was . . ."
You remember your true love spinning at the door.
But you can't remember why.

Life on Earth

—FOR KRYS METZ

House was. Spiteful and
in love house; of water. House blue
as dance a bird   handprint
house.   Play house.
Free to be less
        houseness   straw
and blow down house.
Witness the woods.
Water   house.
Round into a boat stretched
        a boat a girl   there's a red
there on the inside part of a tree
        house   stretched into a ghost house.
Head falling all
        the way through the neck
of the house. Accidental   house
wife gray-haired portion
of a   fun house   of wind in the cold
cold moorings of a boat house   of
mirrors   everything
wet and bending toward
the fully dressed hour
        glass house
Drive by house.
Go to sleep little happiness
                    hat
house.

House a loud toothful
house   had
a shadow curved into
              the blades of a
       back   an outhouse
school house   of God
       of open weight pressing
on the floorboards of the haunted
       girl's lonely paper
              doll house.
The mother house.
       The ma-ma creak of a door
in the dirty cellar's root
house   of healing   to love, water
a wide-eyed walking flesh

was a quiet dead house
       of sticks
that the wind built
accidentally in the wet
    dozing hour of remorse.
Dear house are you a safe house?
A love stretched ghost of a
       house for
babies house of   shadows
       pressing shape into a curved
girl's hands
              house.
A very black and sad patch
       of house   in the hot
house, the choke hold around the neck

                of the family house
call,   house called out into its own roots house
                of grace   house
of mercy house of
blues and blacks between
        the cracks is there a doctor

Field Notes of an Advance Scout: Initiation

My soul changed to a vegetable essence
—FITZHUGH LUDLOW

I'm frightened of becoming
lost, rapt. I feel the foreshadow
doing the listening now. A big flame
happens. Joy hovers, making its trails.
It's making its horse.
My body has a secret eating,
infusion of desert gluten.
It rides its horse through the days.
Spine of cactus is neck of horse.
Angled white horse delivered through spheres,
hauling Maya Deren bone-ghosts
in a hollowed-out pumpkin.
Skin melts, its organ, its cosmic border.
Behind me the cat coils:
pink wheat fluttering
in a boneless hand. A none-wanting.
In my head: abrasion; reversed:
a face arriving as thought.
Coming for me. I have signed
a contract, commenced with the undertaking.
Tipped the cloud for his courtesy.
I open out onto the path.
The long lash of sun
is the shadow of a horse.
We are here, in the middle.
A quiet kind.

There are so many horses but this is my horse.
A woman and a horse and a cactus are one.
A little fire, a little glass field.
A mouth event. My body lumbers.
Dodging hard and sharp things
between movement and space.
We ride toward an idea called
"Apocalyptic Dance Moves for a Cactus."
When its song ends our world ends.
I never even got around to writing the word Love.

2

FLAG IN SPACE

Somewhere
/   along the way

a map fell

out of   my head.
                    This is a flashback,

                        tiny souvenir
                                of my childhood.

I'm a
        part,

            a secret ghost,
                        a spatial souvenir.

        The lost child of so-and-so   /
                                adrift in autumn layers.
                                                    /
Adventure   found me
hiding

            in a crayon.

        I drew the sea:
        red mind, blue crayon,
                    step through.

I'm the boy behind

the shadow of his hand,

the special gray *no* of the dark.

He was   a whim   turned
          wrong

and cleaved to a seascrap
of / God.

Hello boy, I say to / myself.

Shall I pat the hole
where your map fell through?

He /
spills   from my
                               /   making.

His hand,

a voice lamenting.
          We meet in the park   while traversing our self.

He and I: a family group.
          A funny ache.

He shows me
          his sun and I show
                    him mine.

"You are one less   shade of yellow," he says.

                                                        "I have always

been famous"   /   I say.

                        Darkness   converts

         our   loneliness.

We live   /   as parts

                             in   some   air,

oblique and bewildered   faces lodged   on a pole:

CRAYON	SHIPWRECK
GOD	BLUE

Thirteen

Seen through panes:
                the gnomic yard. Many dark
        leapers and couplings, girls removing

sweatshirts for tanks, one boy holds both
                        a hose and a water
        fight in the bunker
                of his age.
They are smoking their incense.
They are exiting their bodies.
        Oh no, there goes another.
Oh no, I broke the lightbulb.

        Hey sorry guys, see you later man.

The entire yard: atomic anthology.
Nothing but air guitar.
        They are massing like larvae.

        Almost every girl is a giant.
        Exiled, we call them treeflowers,
                Giants-who-do-no-dancing.

They are tired of being the slog:
        leaning, burrowing.

Make-out clusters eliminate the yard.
The giants retreat below boughs.
They séance. Scatter an orange-needled circle.

The giants attempt religion
beneath dark-winged pine. Their beanstalk pine,
lifting, flashing its gold. They

interview the dead who deliver
a tall green god. The giants vanish into
its fragrant face, into a devotion
that has nothing to do

with kissing.

Kiss

First we are not kissing you are
just saying it in a bar.
Lights swing loudly.
Twice a second thought seized me almost
entirely out of the room, then
somehow we find each other
the way leaves
find the roofs of houses.
We're a weak-kneed weather map.
We're a cauldron of film noir emergencies.
Summer's first snowfall happens
inside the swarm of our mouths,
each flake rolling like a vowel,
rearranging the molecules
on those two small acres,
our private infinity.
Your snow fills up
my columns my snow
passes your irises like shooting stars,
until our edges implode, tearing
at their corners, undoing
the knots on our shoes.
There is nothing rounder than us,
nothing less upright.
Walls whine for attention
like neglected dogs
and we're snowblind,
mouthfuls of frost, crushed mud.

Dim sounds rise from the earth,
we are dense with sound and buried
in the white zone of ever,
deaf as a tree,
transfixed by this drinkable roar.

Major Arcana

We are having a party called 10-YEAR-OLD SHEE
CHANG FALLS INTO FIRE. I sometimes lie
but no I am not not wasted: we begin
on misfortunate footing at this party, which others
refer to as HOW BIRDS WORK.
Matthew Rohrer performs wearing
George Kalamaras's shoes, later
donned by Engel at BRIAN & VENESSA'S
WEDDING (a.k.a. I AM A MAN OF COLOR).
Within the notion of parallel parties,
Fish and Laird rescue Shee from flames but she
and her bird swoop off through the clockworks.
Silently we all wonder differently about Laird's
wife—*in absentia*—and our thoughts curl
towards each other like sea glyphs. The Beckys W
arrive separately at FREAKED BY MY TEETH.
Melanie tells her IT WAS THE WORST HAND-JOB
EVER! party. Eric smokes four cigarettes but refuses
to get high at CAT PISSED ON DOUG'S COAT.
Doug's in the basement, getting high.
At the bottom of a Budweiser bottle two droplets
revise FRED & LILY MOVE TO NEW YORK
wearing Shee's flaming shoes.
Engel donates his perfect hair to POETRY,
WHY ME? (a.k.a. YOU FUCKING BROOKLYN).
It's the party where Chris Jones confronts
his window in New Hampshire through which John
sees Miss Havisham ("or winter"). We discuss

St. Blaise, patron saint of singers, and I mention
"The name 'Ambrose' means 'immortal.'"
Bill says, "how appropriate for Ambrose Bierce."
Lisa changes her name to "L.A."
then changes it back to Lisa.
Fish says "Anne's son is named Ambrose,"
and Eric recounts an interview in which Anne
credits her son for the "random" part
in *Iovis*. Kelly serves Cossack pie
and plays guitar while Paula sings "Crazy."
The guest of honor surrenders a Pink Moon
at MATTHEW ZAPRUDER FALLS IN LOVE.
Meredith becomes a pantoum.
Juliet's palindrome is both
a palindrome and not a palindrome.
When we say "Anne" we all see the same Anne.
I, however, also see my sister Anne, whose next party
is called THE MOLE ON MY BACK IS A MELANOMA.
Nora is in Milwaukee during SMOKING SALVIA
DIVINORUM when Kevin says "that table
is an exact replica of the town I grew up in!" and
Healey encounters a friendly family of little fears. *Hello*,
they say. Nora is at a party called MY DAD, watching TV.
Steve Burt leaves his Parliaments at THE GOLDEN AGE
OF DOBBY GIBSON. Venessa gets pregnant.
Dobby rides in on his seafoam Vespa.
We finally assume statehood
at ELIOT WEINBERGER'S THREE FAVORITE LIVING AMERICAN
POETS. John says, "Mine is a cloud." Eliot says,
"I never got it about Rilke." Bei Dao waits inside a tulip.
The moon inches above the bracketing hedge.

Meanwhile, Felix Is Born and Brothers Die.
We appear to be indigenous people, all our breaths feel earthy.
There Are So Many Blanks in the World
Where Our Fire Should Be.

3

Field Notes of an Advance Scout: Mutiny

The body of the world, which is broken into pieces,
is the body of a god.
—NORMAN O. BROWN

I offer my body to gravity.
In exchange, gravity offers me
the body which is Mother + Father.
Take, says gravity, *and eat.*
An eating within the eating.

I am your native dragon, says the body.
What I actually see is Mother +
Father climbing out over the rim
of my self into space. Something like
we can't stand the air in here.

My mouth wakes and waters
and wants. I have seen
this dragon before, neither
Mother nor Father but Kingdom.
Captivity. I swallow it whole.

The landscape is lunar and bitter.
I eat through fire to exile, through birth
to bone, through vacuum to sleep,
through mirror to face, and am flung
past Kingdom until Kingdom is merely

a reflection in my thumbnail.
My dragon had a little stutter. My
dragon's eyes were pocky. I am atomic,
and live. I say to that dragon: *Thank
You, Good-bye.* I am rabbit, mountain, tree . . .

Baby Shamanics for the New Millennium

Everybody's pregnant. I myself seem
not to be pregnant most of the time. When
I am, I dream the baby's in a shoe box.
We're all on a plane. The baby is blue.
In the morning mint rises up from me, a fleeing vapor
it flees, has fled. *Mint*. Blue mintine babies
abandoning my lungs like tiny forest people
with tails and spears. I don't know where
they're going, they won't tell me.
They run themselves into a vortex
that tumbles off down the mouth
of an enormous fish.
Do they even know my name?
Can you see what I'm talking about?
I feel like a million luckless heaps of laundry,
all the mint blown out of me.
The basement is musty and mintless,
covered with coughs. Everybody
who's pregnant smokes too much
and must learn to take care of
the babies. Those babies are
blossoming like swirly lupine, their bright
bobbing crowns appearing on Earth
out of nowhere. First there is just us
in the room, then there's a baby.
Sucking and sucking.
So much wetness: the becoming
of things, the letting go, the fleeing pagan babies,

our love our eating our grief.
I am not yet ready to die.
All the onesies in the dryer
I've been saving for our beautiful blue somewhere.

"Straight from New York!"

There's a story you want to tell,
but the party's winding down.
People are sifting through purses
for keys. You may be a little drunk,

but you start anyway then realize
the story's going nowhere, you can't
remember the good parts, whether
the bridge was in Venice or Paris.

Something about desire fastens the story
to your repertoire, something you want
to remind yourself. Like the name of the train
station where a beautiful French man

kissed you on the mouth but didn't
wave from the window though you
waited on the platform and wished you had
noticed the color of his eyes.

An acre of land starts out with desire.
War has desire, fear and swimming have desire.
There are dogs addicted to bee stings.
They wait near late summer garbage

with their tongues hanging out, sweaty
dog tongue-flowers that swell at the onset
of intoxicating seizures. You
want to watch a dog curdle and flop

like a junkie. You want to see a nun
ice skate. You want to see a nun stand
on her impossible head. You want
to inherit a dead nun's shoes. (No,

the story is about Frank Sinatra, violins,
and possibly selling insurance or hosiery.)
You want to go dancing, look sexual.
Then somebody says "You look sexual,"

and you want to become a librarian,
you want to join the Peace Corps. Think
of all the boys who've shot BB's at sparrows,
all the mothers who've lost their sons

in wars. Think of girls
who take razors or paper clips,
slice quiet mouths into their arms.
Watch sparrows spin back and roll

in the gravel like bee-stung dogs, like
Caterpillar Man. He learned how to roll
cigarettes with his lips, light matches,
enjoy a limbless smoke. "It's what I've never

seen before that I recognize," Diane Arbus
said once, and "Freaks are aristocrats." The story
could be said to be about a freak, desire
being its own affliction we wake up with, regretting.

So there's relief, a sweetness
you feel in your gut looking at Hopp
the Frog Boy, Skeleton Dude, Caterpillar
Man, the Mule-Faced Woman. Elastic

Skin Man must have spent hours
at his mirror inventing astonishing habits,
stretching his jaw like putty
when somebody hurt his feelings. Sadness

has desire, little bowls fly around full of jello
and other sad foods. No, the story *is*
about bridges, but the man doesn't jump
and he doesn't play the violin. He sings.

Even when the time seems right
you learn to disrupt the story.
You exaggerate bridges, turn them
into a deck of cards: Bridge of Untuned

Instruments, Bridge of Gypsies
With Too Many Dogs, Bridge
Of Schoolchildren's Pinecones,
Bridge Of A Dull Urge, Bridge

Which Is Path To The Pope.
You want to believe
more than you know,
but sometimes belief makes you lazy.

You can't fathom what a seeing
eye dog sees or what color what he sees is.
He's harnessed, a formless messenger,
ambling like a slow boat toward

his master's invisible home. You retreat
from the story as its details retreat
into shapes your mind can't make
sense of. You daydream a body whose

limbs float away like helium balloons.
A girl makes snow angels, says "These
are my babies." How do you grow up?
How do you crave past safety, into a choice

between chocolate or strawberry, blood
or biscuits, loft apartment or houseboat?
Shaving makes you happy. Hula
hoops don't necessarily make you happy.

There's always something disappointing
in the works, always something amazing
to forget about, always a couch
to lie down on and blather. Well no,

the man doesn't sing exactly but
sort of mumbles Frank Sinatra songs.
He may have sold insurance
from his Brooklyn walk-up.

He may have owned a tobacco shop.
Even now he may be
standing on a bridge
making his pronouncement.

Acts 1

Hours after eating
centuries
we've failed to disrobe
the meatloaf and onions
from our backs.
The restaurant's artistry
has prowled
into our cells,
jeopardized our very style,
our essential presentation!
Also persistent: the bright vision
of wine swaying
in a goblet on the table,
lacking its exquisite goldfish.
We recall an acquaintance
whose new loft apartment
has an indoor pond
and an outdoor pond
in which skewbald koi survive
winter deep below
the frozen scum.
The river in our city
goes unmentioned
most of the time,
its brownness: canals,
ducklings dragged down.
And have you noticed
that flowers—like daffodils—

are shrinking, money's
getting older, almost unusable?
Or a sound you've become
so accustomed to hearing
you don't realize
it's the voice of an owl.
What led us to this restaurant?
What led us to that rock show?
And *God,* the high school
classmate's enormous handbag
in the bathroom at the cinema
where the box on the wall
read "Occidental Exciter."
It's tomorrow and then tomorrow
and we're still alive,
all our faculties about us.
We no longer kiss girls romantically.
Fuzzy lights sharpen.
But now
we've lost track in the restaurant:
the meatloaf,
the meal we share
like a pair of apostles
pleased with their shoes
but not their heaven
nor many of their habits,
a television show they've missed
as a result of this outing,
nor, generally, the music
on the restaurant's jukebox,
and the fact that they will continue to awaken,

shine their faces and drive their cars,
greet their scrappy teeth.
And we don't know
the people who feed us!

4

Because Why

—I.M. LORINE NIEDECKER

Trees are a matter of fact
adorning what? They matter
are sturdy to sit on, are
windy and standing not with.
In fact trees for example.
Those ones, from shifty windows.
Ticking there for stop.
Time to go time
to birth on the hourly snow.
April mattering (Stop) Because
I licked it. Young birch
branch. Rhyme scored
white curled in dirt.
A many birch. I saw
at it, rupture. No,
maple. Here. A skyway
zone because swing. Trees
to pain matter-of-factly.
Bowls upon, clink, ivory
chimes. Carry so much never.
Feel perhaps patriotic, burned,
broken. Sad
to fall and bald and shed.
With standing. Not
per se walking. In fact
we don't certainly know,
perusing only so-called rings.

I remember other than, buffalo
(Heard buffalo? Thunder buffalo?)
Rain, an instant. Mercy
(Whistling. Making wishes.)
("And we'll be jolly friends   for evermore.")
And swings, creaking,
do arouse: trees
matter: to themselves?
Adorning your very own
window yard. Stopbox.
In fact they are (speaking)
simply like thought, as in
like something odd, yarn,
invisible. We can't hear.
What matters in the green
communion because nameless.
Snow, April: we are in fact nameless,
sorry. Perhaps
soothe nothing. I feel
now, only. The Woods.
Are lovely are dark are.
Across my feet the rubbery yard
wet. White. My feet. Trees
too probably stop, cry out.
In fact they may cry out.
Matter of course.
For April is snowing.
Trees do
because
they do because.

Aphasia

The ladies smooth the cloths
and set the salad forks straight.
They slice at loose threads on their bibs: butter knives.
The ladies are knotted like snails.

> *Vera ate Evelyn's pudding.*

> *Was it nice!*
> *Was it nice!*

The ladies at table: slowest eaters alive.
Their hair has been permed.
Their chins have been plucked.
Housecoated, handkerchiefs tucked up their sleeves,
they are stooped and white and spotted.
They are wasp nests dwelling in chairs.

Lawrence Welk's Champagne Music Members
swing smiling from the TV, "I'll Never Smile Again."
M. Corallina won the Easter Coloring Contest.
Stickers on sweaters: "I hugged Ladybug the Clown."
Lou and Lucy, the cockatoos, hoot
around the ward, ricochet.

> *They're all scrubbed,*
> *they all went up.*

"I'll never smile
again / until I smile
at you / I'll never
laugh   / what
good would"

I would chop,
I would drop my

nothing
nothing.

"And the angels swing / and even you'd be
swinging / in my heart, in my heart."

I put it in a box.
My brother had a plane, had a plane, had a plane.

The ladies sleep with their mouths full.
At the back of their throats our epiphany swelters.
They've got the lodestar swinging in their hearts.
A small, small word: did you hear what she said?

My Edward Mary Smoking

is a viola
static & bragging & my
cigarette creeps down
with me my
blue viola
asking "are you happy
w/ two centers"
Smoking too
does
pleasure
the teeth, the silver spit,
a mouth
so heavy
with roundness,
so stuck
like a balloon
it cannot pronounce
the words "word" or
"frog" or "mary viola"
& I/we breathe
& Edward Mary smokes
its viola,
paling
across la la la Why won't
the cross-eyed
viola play
Cannon-ball
They yank them. Elephants

around the sun
Grimacing
our I Edward Marys
decline
behind fog, mirrors
fasten Edward's
blue I to Mary
Why won't it
stop ceasing
la la la

A Hole in the Asp

—FOR PAULA CISEWSKI

Dear P,
The snakes become flowers,
disguise themselves
on rented currents,
find blanks
and settle into
names for unborn babies.

Dear P,
We are mine, arm to ear.
Yours with fingers delivering a garden.
Little voices come from us
circling two gold marbles
in a kitchen bowl, an opaque
womb or funnel or *shhh*
only sometimes
for a moment making its shape,
ripping a slit right here.
We look through with former faces
to the present sky. We choose
the clouds we like best. Those
we gather at a river, we are furtive
and clever. Fertile
when it comes to these clouds.
We call them our dearest memories.

Dear P,
Everywhere you go,
party dresses follow.
How they collect,
think earnestly of you, want
to sparkle your hair!
One night you imagine them
sitting in rows in a boat,
carried away, like nuns.

Dear P,
Why doesn't anyone love the dead babies?
It must not be them.

Dear P,
It is not for the sake of the whole world
that we follow this simple logic.
God sits in a bowl, we bake him.
You accidentally kick
the burning bush and make snow-stars,
each a good twin of a bad leaf.
The impression of the wedding
as vortex, as overflow, is more about
swimming lessons, really.

Dear P,
"I must selectively blossom hurtling
toward the bowl of the gold heart."

5

Dead Babies

1

My nerves are colliding again.
O birds, love me! Dead babies
inhabit the sweetness of all
worlds inside this one.

2

The sky is unfamiliar
with the way dead babies roll over
and play dead. Angels
and dead babies have a thing
or two in common,
such as vertigo.

3

Too many dead babies in one place
will provoke consternation among friends.
Dead babies should be heard but not seen.

4

Dead babies have taken the place
of lost eyelashes, lost socks, lost
waists, lost friends, lost minds, lost roads.
The alchemy of loss is like formaldehyde.

5

In a world where things are going to finish,
my womb bolted away.
Hear swallowed light row into the body,
one dead baby to another.
A kind of migratory prayer.

6

Bushels of dead babies
in the basement. Your high school
ring once lost in your mother's bathroom
now replaces the eye of a dead baby
in a bushel.

7

A terrible face clusters above traffic,
drops its pants like mathematics.
My mother's dead babies are equal
to my dead babies are equal to leaves
rafting the elevated fields.

8

Bicycles in the country accidentally
stumble over the protruding stomachs
of dead babies left for dead on the path.

9

An insolent thought about dead babies
becomes in the mirror a frail shape
precisely the weight of your pulse.

10

Once on the parkway I saw dead babies
hauled around by a clown
in an Astro Van.
Some kids were playing soccer.

11

A shop window in Rome topples
with heads and limbs of plastic
dead babies and owls. On
the street of gold, *compro l'oro*.
Nobody buys the dead babies.

12

A careless coma persists
like the rumor of dead babies dressing
in famous museums.

13

Sometimes a stirring beneath my ribs
reminds me of all the dead babies.
Imagine a bright promise, or surgery.
How quickly they gather in treetops:
the faces of dead babies, your future.

There's a Human Being in the Ditch

A glimpse of lilac (the purple
trick) in the leak the rain made—water-
color collage where tin cans and weepy
yellow grasses, a headlight passing,
cloud, my hand on the car's
window where I'm stopped at a sign—
waver dirtily and tremble with traffic.
You alone are real to me, Rilke said.
He didn't say it to me, exactly.
There's a human being at the bottom
of that ditch, but he's not there.
He's not here. There's a human
being's voice coating the curve
of that cloud, kicking the can,
bringing buckets of lilacs to the door
of my little summer house.
A human being outlined
on the page, chalk outline,
dead person, alone is.
Every word's heart conjures
a terrible casualty. You
mustn't put me back in the cage.
There's a human being
in my ditch, rectangular,
watery, his echo prowls
behind the bricks of this
savagely real, the wakeful
engine of alertness, and animals.

Bridge across Rope

What's not yet history remains opinion.
"*Je ne parle pas anglais.*"
"I think I wish I were dead."

> If I lived in Paris.
> Sound-angles delivered
> through courtyard
> transoms and none
> of it for me.

Here a hat tocks and ticks away.
Hunger eludes the body.
Flowers reverse back into their birthing.

> The peony planted years ago
> so knee-high and thimbly.
> The birch and its ailments.
> A cup, broken, on the stair.
> The whole yard poised in my throat socket
> doing its dying.
>
> > Box of fucking snow.

I encounter my halving.
There I appear, in a piece.
> Here I perish, disperse, burnt leaves.
> What was talk becomes panic and swarms.
> "Please go away."

To be among you like a sheep
vibrating on a wind. Counted,
with a quiet wish for nothing.
The world and its God shrinking
shrinking shrinking shrinking.

God salutes in rusty whispers.
God cackles.

I am bedded down in a thought buzz,
tossed. A little wooden me in my air.

I observe this vow to die, a way.
Turn it over in my hands,
a tin globe. The body's
innards squawk, ripe with birds.
One birdprint brain, red.

What does the mind adore?
(Paris?
A torch song?

)anything silent
anything unlike itself

A shape almost appears
from the ceiling's shadow
as if a flower floated through.

But shapes, too, are deafening.
Time's weed makes mute of me.

Field Notes of an Advance Scout: Torch Song

The greatest secrets lie in regions of danger
—Henry Munn

Wind that is almost abacus.

A green gelatinous wind brain.

Today the medicine surrendered to _____.

Every little part of gravity is upside down.

Do you ever wonder how a wave moves through _____?

The more we move the more we find.

I find my hands carving a _____.

The _____ I ate _____s me.

How the senses sense decides.

Pebbles and chain-link.

Stick letters swum through a childhood.

The childhood drawing a plain black outline.

The child the horse who flew through space.

Our _____ who art in _____.

Here is the symbol for my _____.

I would like to be as _____ in this world.

Something Cinderella. Something very palace.

My precious cactus, you are the Golden _____.

6

Goat Tree

The calendar becomes thin

We reduce sun to tree
          steal it   stand it   choke it
with ropes and bulbs

Then are finished
Then pitch it,

                        Christmas trees flung
                        over a fence for the goats

They line up   The
field a junkyard of tossed
tender shadows

bleating   bristling   night winding
its horn around scenes and snow

Tinsel along with smaller twigs every narrow
needle their rough tongues
are blades as priests   do
                    (sanctified eaters of the dead)

     We reclaim
what the night made different
what eating did   find a pot

for the polished limbs and nail
and hang fish&bows&tin
apples&Easter eggs

Do shapes build
outside a tree   staked to a ghost

We prefer things that stay put take a dead thing
offer it up
                    to the goats   They will make the most
          alter one dead piece at a time

Does the tree remember   Will
the goats   the tree
                    The body knows just where
it's slipping   hears
          wild lights low underground   Softly

its sound grew absent   the trees
lay beside where moonlight shone
          skeletal   Goats
purring and plump   Sweet murmurs

                    (the night thinking the goats had finished)
Green strokes patiently filling their
gullets
                    Inside their chests
a resin climbs and pecks and stiffens them

Bone yard   The sloppy white
ghosts

Myrtle

—FOR THEO PAGE

This time the dream and its leopard fail
to disturb as they might in a genuine slumber.
He seems not and very much "a large ferocious cat."
And the dream's air, which wavers.
Paying attention with synapses where sleep went
missing transforms me into a pine, watching:
the pouting girl thin in her dress.
He chooses not pursuit, but rather sateens
and purrs within her. She inhabits
his wax, its heat, a nest.
I refuse to find a synonym
for the word "hunger," and
the girl may indeed have preferred
a roan mare or a bristly Welsh pony.
The leopard after all blackens
and tooths. Him and his grassy eyesight.

A slippery idea wants to remove me
but part of him leaves to
grow into a violet pulse that rounds
me back to root. His peripatetic soul-
part with the night sky's frail cup his net.
We resume the narrative, the pine and I,
the girl and her leopard. We are
a solid fixture, doing. The leopard holds
up a leaf which becomes a threshold,
cradles the girl in his left cat paw

and slopes over, through. Now it is
simply the leaf of itself, a myrtle.

Am I awake, is this being alive? A medicine man
hands me a bark from my own pine self.

> *The myrtle bears opposite, ovate, lanceolate leaves of*
> *variable width, short-petioled, closely pellucid-punctate,*
> *smooth, glossy, and ever green. It is a Mohammedan*
> *tradition that it was among the pure things carried*
> *by Adam from out the Garden of Eden.*

From far off, a rim of static flashes
like an unghost and my body hangs:
a banquet of total oblivion. Nothing lasts.
The leopard has become a crow,
the girl his beak, then his call. And the call
a ladder I climb as a vine.
Persistently, the "medicine man."
Across the river I can see the leaf in his hand.

> *Myrtle was one of the medicinal plants of the ancients,*
> *practically obsolete in modern therapeutics until revived,*
> *in 1876, by Delioux de Savignac.*
> *The powder, sprinkled upon cotton,*
> *has been applied with marked advantage to uterine*
> *ulceration. Infusion is very unpleasant to take.*

This medicine man does not speak.
Pages of bark become boats he sets to the current,
then turtles, many turtles descending.

He stands on his island.
I am not the girl or the leopard or the myrtle
or the I. Dreams
occasionally happen to the wrong people.
To dream is to risk having someone
else's dream by mistake. When
speech obliterates, when leaves
find the tongue or pucker
to the moist alveoli of lung
and neocortex: one portal
leads to another
and another and he says
it without speaking,
every leaf.

My words don't mean anything I know, they are just seeds,

if I eat them in a row they show me heaven

—Eric Felderman

The Verb *to Plant*

This word grew from the sole of your foot.
First there is a plant, it is just the plant,
it is medicine. *An herb.*
Then it is planted.
To place or set in the ground to grow.
To planter. To bucket the gold.
"The entire plant of the university."
To universe. The entire universe of the plant.
The plants do not live outside.
To set firmly in position; fix.
Is it really called "a plant"?
Any of various organisms of the kingdom
If tree is plant then human must be plant.
Phantae . . . lacking the power
Suddenly we are all planted
in the ground. *of locomotion.*
To flower. (Yes)
I am becoming tree.
A scheming trick; a swindle.
My throat trunk, my head leafy branching.
A person put into place in order to mislead.
The rest of me planted and everyone planted.
To medicine. I tree: we.
Group of buildings for the manufacture of a product.

Each person. Heads above the ground.
To human the plant. *"plant oysters"*
The heads like tombstones but still really heads.
The entire plan of the universe.
Everywhere there are people they are planted people.
Anything that breathes.
To kingdom the human.
Our bodies grow down, glowing white roots.
To fix firmly in the mind; implant.
Stretching wings through sleeves.
To station for the purpose of spying or influencing behavior.
Earth surrenders pathways to us becoming it.
We: often crowded.
Some cannot get sun.
An action in a narrative that becomes important later.
"To change all the way," she plant said.
Our faces contain sun place should enter.
But sun reduce to sunflower.
It spin like pinwheel.
"planted a gun on the corpse to make the death
look like suicide."
Color which liquid wet not.
Place in water or an underwater bed.
We go, through. To through.
To human no longer the Earth.
To were.
"'The rite *of revolution is planted in the heart of man.'"*
In drop we. Entirely to.
The place so as to discover.
And then, we everything.
To deliver [a blow or punch].

It spinning all black conclusion is.
"This," she said, "is what I'm talking about."
To become not becoming any to longer become.
From Latin, planta, *sole of the foot.*

Prosperous Earth

—FOR LAURA RAWSON

A road could lead to San Pedro. On foggy evenings women forage the trenches for certain overgrowths,
collected in aprons and sung over.

MARIA SABINA— WOMAN OF A SACRED AND ENCHANTED PLACE I AM

Could lead an actual man to drag his wooden cross behind him
Women
tall as a doorway, scraping gravel in rough boots.

parting the pavement toward

a meadow where pelicans dive into wild nasturtiums.

There, a hundred Chinese crows are already conscious and speaking.
Whose voices, in unison, sound
like the inside of a leaf.

HIPPOCRATES— FROM THE BRAIN AND FROM THE BRAIN ALONE ARISE OUR PLEASURES

The women evoke a father

    figure, stethoscope. Their songline erases his eyelids. They say *circadia circadia*, sing it.

MEDICATION ROUTES:

inhalation (*ska Maria Divinorum*) or "by use of masks etc"

intra-arterial (*I'm bee stung here*) via hypodermic, medicaments "into an artery" the very heart of me

intracardiac (*an orchestra shot through and nothing but cellos*) oracular mediums obsessively virginal

intramedullary (*alchemical wedding of then with when*) chalky marrow at the farthest opening, and spectral

intrathecal (*lucid drumming, otherwhere phonics are not so brick-like*) subdural space, tap, taps, arise and go now

iontophoresis (*the blue bloating where the feeding took place*) introduction of drugs into a deeper galaxy

sublingual (*la mia lengua campo oscuro*) absorbed through mucosa: walks through walls or on water

In Rome women   On steps as flowers   In fountains as bird figures   In Mexico

    I am a medication route. One of the S's.

Who is root or road. Moving carefully among fruit where shadows and bruises might warn / might warm.

The beginning of twilight is beginning.

Nothing like this lasts long.

Within us the moon might dismantle.

Angelica father's migraines, arthritis, apiaries: grasses colonizing his scalpel

Codonopsis the voice metallic and weaverly (women weaving), skipping a stone up a scope

Polygoni Multiflori our organs are gardens, pick one up, do you love me?

Herba Leonori crimsonly to plural us and kidnap what is dear

Paeoniae Alba the very afterness of a sorrowful hope, skulls knocking about with the ghosts

I CHING— THE WATERS ON THE SURFACE FLOW TOGETHER WHEREVER THEY CAN

I and we are in several places at once now.

Fitful green glossaries killing time. We are sublingual machines. Roads and arteries, a little limp:

one gate is situated along a route on the earlobe.

I met a medicine there. A woman's spirit confronted.

Women at gates, in riverbeds, digressing in the service of transcendence.

Women pulling up roots. They are sturdy unclothed   parting a wound.
The boundaries of the body are ropes, are roads and telescopes. Are muddy.
Are women monitoring the shore for signs of the wheel that moves us.

LINNAEUS— TO LIVE BY MEDICINE IS TO LIVE HORRIBLY

Fire: so many spheres make us itch; contained migration of inquiry.
Earth: a blue attention to inertia, poised.
Water: *nothing like this lasts long* boat in Peiping no the flapping fish no the everness and not breathing.
Metal: synaesthetical sand emerged through a ray.
Air: a surgery performed by clouds for the removal of blank so that trees can.

Probing resembles warfare,
and everything goes: longing, moments, the camps on the body's borders,
                    this season of autumn, these icing-overs of footpaths.

Are not men are not women are

                    flowers in the mouth of that bird.

PLINY— IN SHORT, MAN CAN DO NOTHING AT THE PROMPTING OF NATURE BUT WEEP

Our hands pretend to conceal a teaspoon of sand. It's hard to believe the crows would sing for this.

Or that sleep too has a roof over it, and often we grow misplaced there.

Caught in a bramble: plus the willowy pleasure of elegy

[is there no real survival more distressing than memory?]

Are birds in the flower of this eyelid.

A jar of foggy overgrowth:

• The furry sea
• The prosperous medicament chamberhood
• The trembling split-open arrival of boulders replaced by infants
• Smoke slurring across our livid contours
• The mask of distance evolving into fabric
• Touches accumulated in bureaus just beyond reach
• The cavernous glossaries of dissolution and singing
• This train is bound for a place called gone
• The moon   *um*   and its negative?

77

HUANG TI— WHEN THE DEATH PULSE OF LUNGS ARRIVES, IT SHOULD APPEAR LIKE A FLOATING
OBJECT OR LIKE A HAIR BLOWN BY THE WIND

A wall where not gates nor doors through which swimming remains our only option.
Wall that resembles body or *here*. Wall within wall without and within every wall presently to know.
At a certain point the breath must learn to adapt to its absence.

JESUS— I SEE MEN AS TREES, WALKING

The earth, this one place where we live.

I met a plant there.
When we meet again we will kiss for the very first time.

MARIA SABINA— THERE IS A WORLD BEYOND OURS, A WORLD THAT IS FAR AWAY, NEARBY, AND INVISBLE. . . .
THAT WORLD TALKS

Pulling up roots, morning glories, a singing: which they eat.
And become swans.

7

How Birds Break

Blessed be the birds for they will be blown
away and burned. Multiplied
by the first language of wind,
abandoned nests cling to elastic branches.
Vibrating, vegetal. An ice-blue
trill cramps with a prodigal twilight.
What is the ration?
Charred midflight. Bones.
Swept sparrows lit at the altars
in blessed leafy gutters.
Left at the steps with a lidful glare.
Pink in them. Spices. Our hearts
swell with a feeling of finished
wings, at last we revere them
utterly. Flying
into caves. They have air
to make sounds with, to soar on,
then they do not have it
any longer. Blessed
be the nimble sound of a crow.
Birds batting at the door and in hair,
blessed be the blight we
flee from. A thousand birds
skewed east like divers poised
at the rim. Blessed be the hysterical
utterance of sound in the mouths
of creatures. Clocks yet stopped
at the very hour, finches flying past

explode within that round conclusion.
A solitary dove then swoons
into circles of absentia
so brief it's silver.
Feeds the bits of calendar back to its worm.
Each wind begins with the arrival
of birds. Such a metallic
fur on our skyline. Blessed
for we love them though they will not
stop to save us. Yes
an intimate future leafs through
our fingers, flies off. *Think of how tired*
their little wings. Caught in the eye
of a storm they ended up mistakenly.
The gauzy cut-outs, have you ever autopsied
a bird? Had papery x-ray
daydreams? An obstinate palsy
hangs over the people. How many
trees on this horizon? How do they choose
where to land? Smoke.
Endless fields of flutter, hawing.
Cooing. The low-flying pigeons
clothed with the sun, their stupid labor.
Smudges of poverty become bells
tied to their skinny talons.
Is it sad that babies cannot
distinguish a bird from a plane?
Blessed be the babies, with eyes full of wing.
Fallen, fallen. Write this down:
happy are the dead.
Their hum won't be returning.

The little beating, beyond terrains of sound,
little efforts. Blazes resembling
documents. The beloved's wings
empty over a heaviness, a night of
no one sleeping. Pray for the lack,
blessed be anguish. The clouds
part so politely for this spectacle.
Here is the quickening cluster,
or are we still watching TV?
Blessed be levitation
for it shall yield a downpour.
Scald-crow, raven, carrions,
laser-browed hawks, street
roosters, swallows, the blood
dart of cardinals, gaggles, bastions and rookeries,
ostriches striding the desert, the hummingbird—
how we esteem each blessed delicacy.
Was there anything like a ghost
in their tilting? So early in the fever,
the fable of fury and wings
unfolding before the advancing night.
Does it hurt to crash down from the sky?
Blessed be the phantom limb of destiny.
Do you know you are glad you were born?

Geodesy

I'd witnessed stories of batless and bangs
all flung headlong into a broken heart.
Memory happened, descending the staircase
accidentally—drowning, say,
which doesn't mean disapproved.
I could no longer be loved.
Ajar on a hot stone,
I dreamed I was not a snake.
Flying flying over friendly fields.
The sky my hair and won the war.

I awoke with a huge prying hunger.
My mother liberated
a monster disguised as a flood.
I could not abandon the beginning
though others gave in, disobeyed.
On the seventh day we wept
heartily, our kneecaps shattered.
It was as if we had nothing to
live for, ever. A woman
reclined naked on the knoll and I
could not recognize I am, or was.
In an embrace toward half
asleep, sound opened, pressed
and unloading into morning.

A thousand years later I find myself
here on a wooden chair writing
my dispatch in the pre-dinner rush
for you. Thank God
we're still around to see all of this?

Everybody Loves Eric Dolphy

—FOR BRIAN ENGEL-FUENTES

Father glues the hippo back
together, as he's done before
when the others broke.

It's no small task.

Opened envelopes hang
like cranes on a line. Herons,
in real life, are bigger but hard

to make with a piece of paper.

When Elvis died, nothing
happened to the weather. Nectar
toured the planet, nesting

in the mouths of bees.

A cello murmurs something
about tennis, or sailing.
Only the walls know for sure—

they're so discreet!

Days are short here, nights
shorter. We sleep
like blind sailors in beds

that deliver us secretly home.

Field Notes of an Advance Scout:
Transubstantiation

In such fearsome circumstances / this strange fate befell me . . .
—MILAREPA

In this vision, the sage Milarepa
lies on a cliff in the snow with his cloth,
having a thought that speaks Mayan.
The thought is an x, the foxes are barking.
The cactus has named itself "Milarepa."

"I have no home in any place."

An Advance Scout loves like a savage
nun loves, chanting her lover through space:

> *Bronze Tools,* says.
> *Courtly Love,* says.
> *Lightbulb,* says.
> *Microchip,* says.

"Knowing all things I comprehend them to be one."

I find a love sound at the crossroads,
essence of animal captured in x.
From each of its limbs wander tiny *Pre-me's.*
At its center, an event called *Cells.*
At its negative, a song called *You May Never
Be Patient Enough To Know Where A Cactus Is Going.*

*"That I am the singer of little songs / proves
that I have learned to read the world as a book."*

8

The Whole Desert Island Scenario

I'd bring the short, or the long
Japanese kimono and that Max
Ernst book if it pleases you.

I imagine fine tropical spreads.
Nights making flutes under the stars,
nights fiddling with the flutes we've made.

Naturally there'd be hardship,
but we'd split the difference
by mastering unusual vocations

(sand art, French braiding, contortionism).
Perhaps you'd tell me at long last
how you came to be so famous.

Eventually a tawny
shape would grow up
from a clutch of buried hair.

The grave would yawn
from its furry parish and entertain us
with glow-in-the-dark coils and tantrums.

You'd repeat every syllable you've uttered.
As for me, my life story is long
and mostly untrue. We needn't bother.

In fact I'm still here, it's the same old house.
The cavity between thunder and lightning
informs me a storm's approaching.

Trees phrix and totter.
Portraits and receipts skim
the gutters, there for the taking.

I remember the time my father
took me on his knee, told me
"it's better to keep your mouth shut."

Testimonial documents pile up
in the basement's secret room,
now flooded. Veins of ink

seep from under the door,
revealing the extent of my effort.
I'll grab for whatever rushes by.

To Win a Wife

The end of the path is the beginning
of the flower. One day, arrive early.
Dawn stands before you with its dark salts.

A thought thinks you.
Its sky hurts your eyes.

The crows will seem to enslave you,
pretend to warn you.
Peck at your neck for a coin.

Pay attention.

Anyway they are just crows.
Your fortune is further than crow.

What was bear about you becomes fish,
treading the grass. Lumbering
with your floaty eyes.

If an eye falls out,
feel the grass transform it
to a blue stone the size of your navel.
It is not always bad to lose sight of the world.

You may ask yourself: *Who made me?*
Furthermore: *Couldn't I have a horse?*
Not this time.

A stinging nettle directs you
toward the forest, and in your pain you
make a god happen.

Invent yourself a horse:
Soft nuzzle on your cheekbone.
Tail swatting crows from your neck—
oops, it knocked out an eye.

The name the crows spelled out on
the sky has dispersed among bees.
Has moistened the lips of the honeydippers.

This mountain must be a mistake!
The map in your hand becomes a scar;
now it's a mirror—
your own reflection reveals nothing.

You could have felt happier being a bear,
or even a fish. Now the horse is only imaginary.

When thought thinks of you,
the image slips a little.
So it goes, advancing through space.

Why must the horse lie down and die here?
Where are the crows when you need them?
Movement in time makes a fuzzy poison.

At last you arrive at the river.
When night falls deep into its zero,
You'll constantly awaken a bride.

Last Minute Details

My husband is husband of wheelbarrows
& roller rinks, husband of foreign policies,
husband of manatees & headlights, bourbon.
It's night I'm looking for the captain of a ship.
Two rocks like little thrones appear
to me from a city of rocks.
A breeze sweeps an ash from my hair. My husband
is husband of keyholes, elderberries,
Cubist nudes. Husband of moons & eclipses.
My husband is husband of birch trees & swings
& boys bending branches & the earth
the right place for love. Husband
of clouds. He's not
a sailor but we're sipping
champagne, lounging on Victorian sofas.
There is no captain of a ship, there are two
rocks only. Grass stains on his knees.
His hair falls into my face, he breathes
an empire into the river-worried, calico
night. My husband
is husband of blue the color,
artichokes, radio signals, glass slippers,
husband of luck. Husband my husband
of each beautiful woman
& mothers & history & silent movies,
husband of waterfalls,
husband of night's strings dangling
stars flat as lit plates on the water.

Grass on our backs. We're two
stars our hair falling into the night,
river mouthing juried names like
indivisible we are *revenant* we are *rapture.*
My husband of my two hands two
husks opening, my inventions,
my every harvest & inclination, grass,
my rowing away from the rest of it
toward & toward & toward him.

We Are Making (Cat Outdoors)

caution rises
to lull the Sunday
wheel's evening wheel
hurrying up the sea, heaving
at evening toward where

metal flames fall down,
waking arcs of white
logic to make new who?

                              small bird please don't
                                 step down here   now

make dark children,
even as machinery
in the shadow of a sound
                              (small outline of a bird)
coming,

gathering younger parts
plus white joy
plus space   body

                 itself falls

birds
rain sleep
rain birds and night
float darkly children
walk their boots to heaven

                                        (fallen

                                                bird)

reeling ghosts white in
the arc of

                        me you we
dead bird
red head dead
quiet on the floor

                                                (very here

                                                on the rug)

heroes animate machines
and sleep
and the history of hair

                                (or very young bird, quiet finch)
cupped by white hands
the face of the hands' once ago

                                (finch of the once-ago ate

                                                here)

there!   today there buds
sexually green on the twigs

                                        (clattering, cheeping)

        this bird

but one must go for the other to
come
come shine come wheel right in now
fly sea back to the
sea, come here now

9

Imagining Girls

A difficult display waiting in that very
small room I don't remember. Movement, like
bodies of a wide field closing vacantly into water.
Blinding down her charming hands
my skin rolled nearly as music.
        As if my eyes would like to be dead.

We woke liberally, different.
I won't hum. For dreams the long night opened
a sadness. Merely a kiss? My belly warming by then.
And the fool, stooping

, trapped herself   myself
a discontinuous creature, a duplicate of:
silver people, of pity, of merely opposite girls
who minister, reverse loneliness. Merely.

A great vocation imagines the hectic in a presence.
Cold girls, their wild honey membranes.
Wore white, untie, a gift.
Perching, perching, *I'm a flower.*
Very sort of wedgelike.

        [—Imaginable daughter—]

                        (his)

Sheer, it's impossible to glimpse her!
How translate what's left in the space of what leaves?

My own daughter: golden stalk here on the porch.
Touch her, she's precisely here. So many girls!
Here and there.
So many girls gone missing.

Look: this inarticulate prayer skitters about me.
Our hats were nothing frivolous and despite my sparkle I am
    also a basket.
Things can grow in me.
Things can grow on me.
There are too many girls here?
Finding my lips but not my beloved.

I can't swallow a thing!
We will have a garage sale and disburse our love.
For the girls are forgiven

                                   (forgotten?)
, daughters swell in their own safety.
We are sheer but precisely here, touch us.
I imagine voices in great numbers
and sins clothed in gold, in blue frocks.
I imagine, my love, but you happen to be.
Heaven was made for them.
The low earth finds me again. The low earth.
The low and present belly of the Earth.

How to Get the Love You Want

Hold my whispers.
I have the impression that Father
hauls his dusk through aisles
of bent-up crows. The horse's
shadow canters sidelong
up the gate, into the neighbor's
plum grove. His ears twitch
at snowflakes as if at
bitter flies, as if unfastened.

Truth is plain.
Like a little house
between heaven and earth.
A horse in the yard.
Crows on the roof.
Snow heaving against the doorway
like grown men hoisting a wall.
Inside the house Father multiplies.
Mother mends the baby over the fire.

Darkness could resist me,
could slip
past the faces of strangers.
Become stained.
I ride the horse into the woods,
chasing the wheel as it goes.

It is unimaginable to be a horse,
isn't it? Or a wheel, to be never
upright for long. I lope
from fire to fire. Hope
whispers through its stain.

Field Notes of an Advance Scout: Impersonation

Come pray with me, my sister / to recover vegetable permanence
—EDMOND VANDERCAMMON

I am a mourning, mounting woman
A woman who nourishes among the birds and the house creatures
A woman I am who feeds the flame of a dragon
Who   plants
To plant woman
A tall and owl bright woman
She is an owl, a wind-in-tree woman
Ovum-off-the-hook woman
Woman of a birthing noise   we are
Woman of soft hum   pushing   we are
Woman of lost joys
Effigy woman
Made-from-birds woman
Quiet woman, says
Our hard road woman
Our bird woman of aqueducts and riverbanks
Our nesting swan woman
Good-at-sleeping woman
A woman I am full of a hoop woman
She is a mirror woman
Woman-who-makes-a-horse-happen

The Book of Fortunes Begins at the End of Itself

Set your crown
on the shore and holster
your face. Its smaller
version can't measure

your shoulders running
the length of the river but
some place trembles
in the wounds of disappearance.
That is why it only rains a little.

And constantly re-invents
the clouds we cannot captivate.

I think of you, buying bones
to measure your songs,
glancing birds in each day
ours was. To you, only not too much today.

At the top of the shoulder bells
warn small creatures of approach so to not
inadvertently step on one of them.

We can't hang the stray
feelings from their ankles in trees
to make things beautiful
or appear not to perish.

favorable to riches and spying.

I came out and coughed
up my part in the crime.
I showed you the box,
opened its paper people,
their limp dancing.

We went curdling onto the streets
dreaming *a lithe awakeness.*
"I" a mere metaphysical—small
disgrace—its brave
horizon rocking into a cup
of kissing.

Our heads have not severed
or plummeted through
weather too round for
the face of a bird.
From then on.

a small day spoke back joy
to a wind we polished
and believed. It changed
the syntax of our life. Spliced
people into birds, their perfect
spheres disappearing into the lack of a cup.

Happiness is a useful detail.
We watch ourselves require
translation: *Here is a live coal from an alphabet.*
It carries the code of our cloudsong. *It will polish
how happy you are.* We carry
back the syntax of our perfect spheres
everywhere thinking *favorable
to riches and questions.*

Colophon

Because Why was designed at Coffee House Press in the historic warehouse district of downtown Minneapolis. The text is set in Minion.

Funder Acknowledgments

Coffee House Press is an independent nonprofit literary publisher. Our books are made possible through the generous support of grants and gifts from many foundations, corporate giving programs, individuals, and through state and federal support. This book received special project support from the National Endowment for the Arts, a federal agency, and from the Jerome Foundation. Coffee House Press receives general operating support from the Minnesota State Arts Board, through an appropriation by the Minnesota State Legislature and from the National Endowment for the Arts. Coffee House receives major funding from the McKnight Foundation, and from Target. Coffee House also receives significant support from: an anonymous donor; the Buuck Family Foundation; the Bush Foundation; the Patrick and Aimee Butler Family Foundation; Consortium Book Sales and Distribution; the Foundation for Contemporary Arts; Stephen and Isabel Keating; the Outagamie Foundation; the Pacific Foundation the law firm of Schwegman, Lundberg, Woessner & Kluth, P.A.; the James R. Thorpe Foundation; the Archie D. and Bertha H. Walker Foundation; TLR/West; the Woessner Freeman Family Foundation; and many other generous individual donors.

To you and our many readers across the country, we send our thanks for your continuing support.

Good books are brewing at coffeehousepress.org